The big 5
and other wild animals

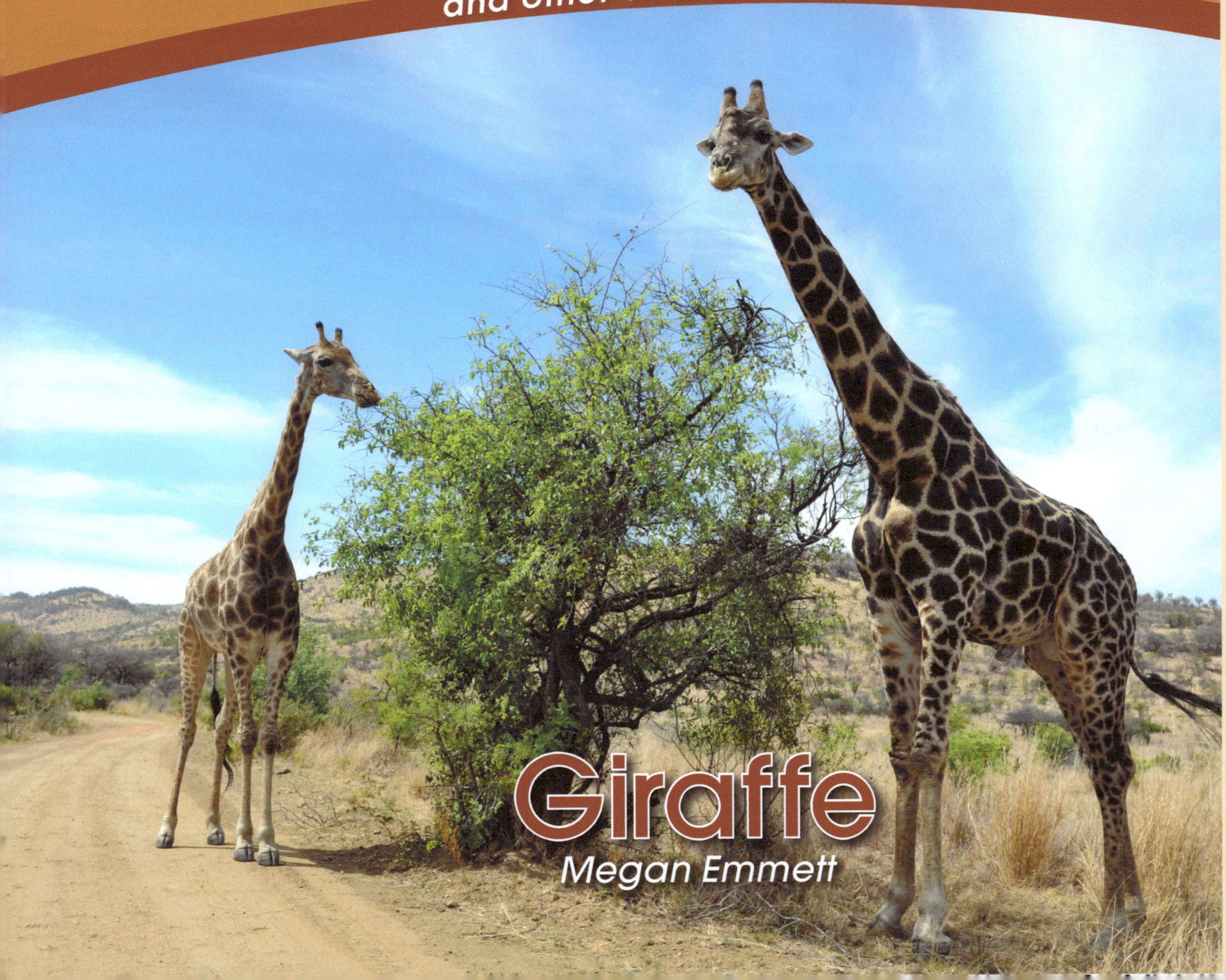

Giraffe
Megan Emmett

The big 5 and other wild animals series is published by
Awareness Publishing Group (Pty) Ltd.
Copyright © 2019

Awareness Publishing (SA) (Pty) Ltd
www.awareness.co.za
info@awareness.co.za
+27 (0)86 110 1491
www.facebook.com/AwarenessPublishing

All rights reserved. No part of this publication may be reproduced in any form without written permission from the publisher, except by a reviewer.

First edition, 2019

Giraffe by Megan Emmett
ISBN 978-0-6393-0008-5

Summary: An introduction to the giraffe, a wild animal. This book looks at the giraffe's physical characteristics, its eating habits, its family life and the ways it communicates. The book also talks about the conservation of giraffes.

Book design: Dana Espag and Bianca Keenan-Smith.

Editorial credits: Educational consultant: Gillian Mervis. Copy editor: Danya Ristić. Proofreader: Lynda Gilfillan. Picture editor: Anne Laing. Indexer: Lois C Henderson.

Illustrations: Cartoons: Gerhard Cruywagen of Greenhouse Cartoons, and Dana Espag. Additional drawings: Dana Espag.

Photo credits: Cover and pp.3 (top and middle), 6, 7, 8, 9, 10, 11 (bottom), 16, 30 (left), 36, and 40 © Anne Laing; p.3 (bottom) © lightpoet / Shutterstock; pp.4 and 15 © Megan Emmett; p.11 (top) © Lenice Harms / Shutterstock; p.12 (left) © 333DIGIT / Shutterstock; pp.12 (right),18, 20, 22, 28, 29, 30 (right) and 42 © Shem Compion; p.13 © Matt Ragen / Shutterstock; p.14 (top) © Dr_Flash / Shutterstock; (bottom) © DLILLC / Great Stock / Corbis; p.23 (left) © Karel Gallas / Shutterstock; (middle) © SoopySue / iStockphoto; (right) © stobi_de / iStockphoto; p.24 © Mogens Trolle / Shutterstock; p.26 © AfriPics; p.32 © Liga Alksne / Shutterstock; p.33 © Roy Toft / National Geographic / gallo Images; p.34 © Masterfile / Great Stock / Corbis; p.38 © Felix Mizioznikov / Shutterstock; p.39 (left) © Frans Lanting / Great Stock / Corbis; (middle) © dawnn / iStockphoto; (right) © MarcLSchauer / Shutterstock.

You can read more by Megan Emmett about animals in the book *Game Ranger in Your Backpack – All-in-one Interpretative Guide to the Lowveld*, published by Briza Publications (2010, Pretoria). ISBN 978-1-920217-06-8.

1 3 5 7 9 0 8 6 4 2

Contents

Quick facts	5
Meet the giraffe	7
The giraffe's coat	9
Males and females	13
Reaching the leaves	15
The giraffe's mouth	17
Strange eating habits	19
Drinking	21
Living together	23
Neck-fighting	25
"Follow me" sign	27
Baby giraffe	29
Staying out of trouble	31
Helping other animals	33
Making a noise	35
How giraffe and thorny trees both stay healthy	37
Relatives	39
Conservation	41
Glossary	43

A side view of a male giraffe, showing his long legs and long neck.

Quick facts

Height	Male: 4–5,5 metres tall Female: 3,5–4,5 metres tall
Weight	Male: 900–1 400 kilograms Female: 700–950 kilograms
Lifespan	About 25 years
Gestation (pregnancy)	15 months
Number of young	One at a time
Habitat	Open bushveld where there are leafy trees to eat; sometimes forests in the bushveld; the desert. They do not live high up on mountains
Food	Leaves, fruit and flowers
Predators	Lions and hyenas
Interesting fact	Giraffe are the only hoofed animal with two toes that have a gestation longer than one year
Is it one of the Big Five?	No! But it is the tallest wild animal and one of the biggest animals in the bush

Words that appear in the text in bold, **like this**, are explained in the Glossary at the end of this book. Some key words are in colour.

The giraffe's bones

It might seem strange, but the giraffe has the same number of bones, or vertebrae, in its neck as a mouse! Giraffe and mice, and even people, are mammals. All mammals have seven vertebrae in their necks. Mammals are creatures whose babies grow inside their bodies. And mammal babies drink their mothers' milk when they are born.

Giraffe are tall enough to reach and eat leaves at the top of trees.

Meet the giraffe

Giraffe are the tallest animals in the world. Giraffe have long legs and a long neck. Because they are so tall, giraffe can reach leaves that are high up in trees. No other animals, except big elephants, can reach leaves that are so high.

Scientists use **Latin** names for animals, so that scientists who speak different languages can all use the same name for each animal. The giraffe's Latin name is *Giraffa camelopardalis*, and *camelopardalis* means "camel-like leopard". This name describes the giraffe well because the giraffe's fur, or coat, is the same colour as the coat of a leopard. The giraffe's coat is gold in colour, with brown patches. The leopard has a gold-coloured coat with black spots.

And a giraffe has a similar walk to a camel. The giraffe first moves its two legs on the left side, then it moves its two legs on the right side. The giraffe walks like this to stop its long legs from getting caught up in each other. In this way, it avoids tripping. The giraffe's long neck also helps to keep the giraffe balanced.

A male giraffe, with the brown patches on its fur that every giraffe has.

A giraffe's coat is made up of patches, and the patches are slightly different shapes and shades of brown.

The giraffe's coat

A giraffe's coat is covered with brown patches. Every giraffe's coat has its own pattern of patches, so no giraffe ever looks the same as another giraffe.

The patches on the giraffe's coat help the giraffe to hide from **predators**. The pattern of brown patches looks similar to leaves and shadows in the bush, so when the giraffe stands still, the patches blend in with the bushes and trees. Even though the giraffe is so tall, other animals may not see it when it stands still. This blending in with the bushes and trees is the giraffe's **camouflage**, and it stops the predator or enemy from seeing where the giraffe is hiding.

The patches become darker as a giraffe gets older. Old male giraffe, or bulls, sometimes have patches that are almost black. The patches on the coat of a male giraffe become darker than those of female giraffe.

The pattern of patches on its coat helps the giraffe to blend in with its surroundings.

The coats of these young giraffe, on the left and at the front, will darken as they grow older.

The giraffe's coat continued

There may be differences in the coats of giraffe, depending on where these animals live. Giraffe living in one area may have light, or pale, coats, while the coats of giraffe living in another area may be darker. There are two reasons for this. First, giraffe in different places eat different food, and the food that they eat affects the colour of their coats. Second, some areas are hotter or colder than other areas, and this difference in the air temperature can affect the colour of the giraffe's coat.

An example of a reticulated giraffe's patches.

Giraffe in different parts of Africa

Giraffe that live in different places have different-looking coats. For example, the reticulated giraffe, which lives in northern Kenya, has large patches of similar shape. The patches are all orange-brown, and have thick white lines between them. The southern giraffe lives in southern Africa, and its patches are smaller and have different shapes. Some of the patches are in the shape of stars. The background is light brown, and the patches go down the legs to the hooves.

An example of a southern giraffe's patches.

The male giraffe has two horns on his head, and there is no hair on top of each horn. He also has a big bump in the middle of his forehead.

The female giraffe has horns that are thinner than those of a male, and they are hairy on top.

Males and females

Both male and female giraffe have horns, called ossicones, but the horns do not look exactly the same. The horns of a male have no hair on the top – they are bald. A bull's horns are also thicker than those of a female. Female giraffe, or cows, have thinner horns. They also have a bunch or tuft of black hair, like a paintbrush, on the tip of each horn.

Bulls have a big bump in the centre of their forehead. This is like a third horn, and it is called the median horn. Every time a bull bumps his median horn during a fight, it gets bigger. By the time the bull is old, his median horn is quite large. Fighting also causes other knobs and bumps to appear on the bull's forehead.

A bull's coat has darker patches than a female's coat. Bulls are also taller, sometimes by a metre.

Bulls (left) are darker and taller than the cows (right).

Giraffe are browsers, and so they eat tree leaves.

A female giraffe, watched by her calf,
bends down to eat the leaves of a bush.

Reaching the leaves

Giraffe are **browsers** – they eat leaves. The giraffe's long neck gives it an **advantage** over other browsing animals in two ways. First, the giraffe has a better chance of reaching the leaves that are highest on trees. Elephants, by using their long trunks, are the only other browsers that can reach leaves as high. Second, when food is scarce, most browsing animals struggle to find enough food to eat. Giraffe have a better chance of finding food because they are able to reach the highest leaves.

Bulls are much taller than cows. The tallest bulls reach almost six metres high! Because bulls are taller, bulls and cows feed at different levels on a tree. Bulls stretch their necks to feed from the top of the tree, while cows bend down a little and eat leaves that are lower. So bulls and cows do not have to share food with each other, and there is enough food for them all to eat.

Mr Giraffe, the gardener

When giraffe eat, they often change the shape of trees. Even a giraffe cannot reach the top of a very tall tree, and so it eats the leaves around the middle part of the tree. The tree may end up looking as if it has a waist – it will have a fatter part at the top, a thinner part in the middle where the giraffe feeds, and a fatter part at the bottom.

The giraffe uses its pointy lips and long tongue to eat leaves off a thorny tree.

The giraffe's mouth

Giraffe eat the leaves of trees and of other plants. Some of the plants from which they feed are thorny. The giraffe has special physical features, called **adaptations**, that stop its face, mouth and tongue from being hurt or damaged by the thorns.

One adaptation is the giraffe's eyelashes. They are very thick and long, and they protect its eyes from being harmed by thorns, twigs and leaves. When the eyelashes touch anything, the eyelids close and the eyes are not harmed. Another adaptation is the giraffe's long tongue. The tongue is 45 centimetres long, and the giraffe can push it far out of its mouth. The giraffe can reach leaves that are above its head with its long tongue. The giraffe can eat all the leaves on a branch by wrapping its tongue around the branch and pulling the leaves off. But it can also carefully pick off one leaf at a time and eat it.

The giraffe's tongue feels like rubber and is covered with sticky saliva, or spit. The tongue is also covered with rough little bumps called papillae (puh-PIH-lee). So the tongue is tough and slippery, and thorns cannot easily prick it.

A third adaptation is that the giraffe has a thin, pointy face and its upper lip moves easily. Just as we use our fingers to do something carefully, the giraffe uses its lips to carefully remove leaves from between the thorns.

Giraffe sometimes eat soil or bones. When they eat these things, they have to bend down very low to do so.

Strange eating habits

Sometimes, giraffe eat unusual things, such as bones or soil. Eating bones is called osteophagia (os-tee-oh-FAY-ja), and eating soil is called geophagia (jee-oh-FAY-ja).

Giraffe have extremely large **skeletons** in their large bodies. Their long necks and their long legs are made up of big bones. The leaves that giraffe eat do not always give them enough of the minerals, or salts, that they need to keep their bones strong. Two minerals that giraffe especially need are calcium and phosphorus. During winter, leaves have little calcium and phosphorus. But soil and bones almost always contain these minerals, and so giraffe eat soil or bones in the winter months, and during times of not much rain. If giraffe are living in areas of poor soil, then they will get these minerals by chewing bones.

When giraffe eat soil and bones, they have to bend their necks down to lick the ground or pick up a bone. They also have to bend their necks down when they drink water.

Giraffe have difficulty drinking, as they have to spread their long legs sideways to get low enough to reach the water.

Drinking

Giraffe get most of the liquid that they need from the leaves that they eat. They also drink water, every two or three days, if there is water in the area.

Because the giraffe has a long neck and long legs, it has to bend down low when it drinks. To reach the water, a giraffe must spread its front legs wide apart and then lower its head. When its mouth reaches the water, the giraffe drinks quickly and then stands up again. Giraffe are **vulnerable** when they bend down to the water – they cannot protect themselves properly from predators. So they usually drink quite quickly.

When a giraffe bends its neck to drink water, all the blood in the neck could rush down and flood its brain. To stop this from happening, giraffe have special blood vessels in their necks.

At the bottom, or base, of the giraffe's head there is a group of tiny veins that work like a sponge. When the giraffe bends down, the veins close, and only small amounts of blood can flow through the veins. When the giraffe stands up again, the spongy veins stop the blood from flowing back through the neck too quickly. If the blood flows too quickly, the giraffe could feel dizzy.

The giraffe's heart

When a giraffe is standing up, its head and brain can be as high as five metres above the ground, and almost two metres away from its heart. The giraffe has a big heart – big enough to pump blood up its long neck to its brain. The giraffe's heart weighs ten kilograms, and pumps 60 litres of blood every minute!

Giraffe change groups regularly, and do not live in family units.

Living together

Giraffe live alone, or in groups with other giraffe. Many animals live in family groups, but giraffe are different. Giraffe live in **temporary associations**, which means that they do not stay in the same groups for long – they change their groups often. Within a few hours, the giraffe in a herd or large group may have changed many times.

There are no close bonds, or relationships, between the giraffe in a herd. Only mothers and their small babies, called calves, have a close bond. When the calves are old enough to look after themselves, the bond between the mother and her baby weakens.

Giraffe that are of a similar age often stay together in a herd. Young male giraffe, called bachelors, tend to group together. Calves may all stay together in a group called a crèche (KRESH). Male and female giraffe of all ages can be found together.

Two bulls neck-fighting.

Neck-fighting

Giraffe bulls usually live alone. They may join up with giraffe herds, but they stay only if there is a cow that is ready to mate. When a cow is ready to mate, we say that she is in heat, or in **oestrus** (EE-striss).

Giraffe bulls do not have their own **territories** – many bulls may live in the same area. When bulls meet one another, they do not fight. From an early age, all the bulls in an area play together and they know which bull is the biggest and strongest.

When two young males, or bachelors, meet each other, they play-fight with their necks. We call this necking. The giraffe try to hit each other on the neck with the top of their bony horns. As one giraffe tries to hit the other, the other giraffe moves away and does not get hurt. Necking *looks* slow and graceful – the giraffe look as if they are being blown by the wind. But the bachelors are actually practising for fights they will have as adults, when the blows can be quick and powerful.

Older bulls sometimes fight over cows that are in heat. The two bulls start by necking, but then the fighting may become serious. The blow can be very painful if one bull hits the other hard enough with his horns. The other bull's neck or body may be injured. One of the bulls will eventually give up.

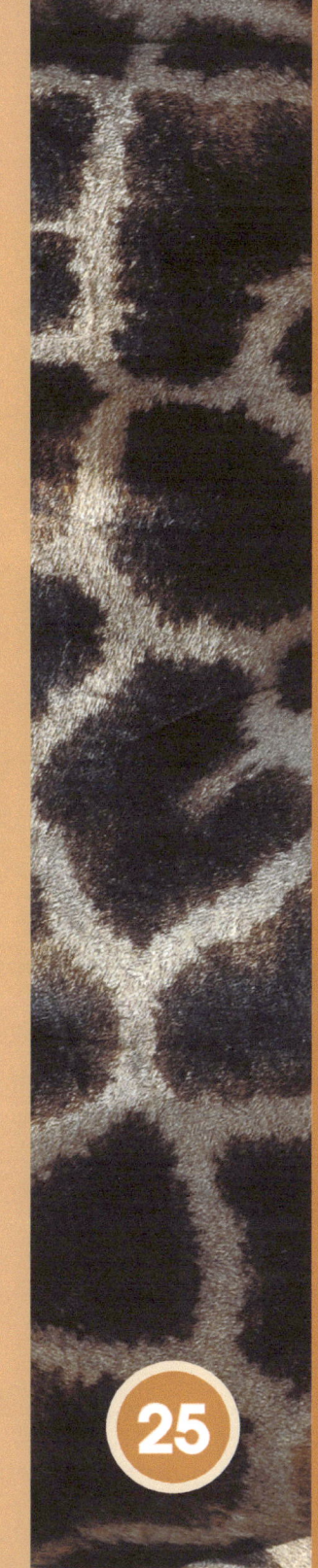

The back of a giraffe's ears is white, so that other giraffe can easily see it.

"Follow me" sign

When a giraffe wants to join up with a herd, it is easy for it to find one. The giraffe has good eyesight, and it can spot other giraffe from far away because they are so tall.

Giraffe have white skin behind their ears. This skin looks bright, which makes it easy for giraffe to find each other. Giraffe can see this white skin from a distance, even if they cannot see the rest of the other giraffe's body.

The white skin is a "follow me" sign – it helps giraffe to find and follow each other.

Giraffe calves lie down to rest and to hide from predators.

Baby giraffe

A baby giraffe, or calf, weighs about 100 kilograms. A calf can stand when it is only 15 minutes old.

Giraffe are extremely tall animals. But when a calf is born, it does not fall a long way to the ground. At the start of the birth, the calf's head appears, together with its front legs. The mother bends down so that the calf's feet touch the ground. This makes sure that the calf will not fall and be hurt when the rest of its body comes out.

Newborn and young calves spend much of the time lying down and hiding in long grass. While a calf is hiding in the grass, it grows and becomes stronger. The mother stays close to her calf most of the time. She protects it and feeds it on milk from her teats. We call this suckling. While the mother is away feeding, the baby knows that it has to stay hidden. It may even put its neck down if a predator is nearby, so that the predator will not find it.

When calves get older, they all stay together in groups or crèches for their protection. One mother guards and takes care of all the calves. The other mothers can then go off to find food.

Born with horns

Giraffe calves are born with horns, but the horns are not yet joined to their skulls. The horns are soft, and they bend easily so that the calf does not get stuck when it is being born. As the calf grows, the horns join to the skull and become solid bone.

Running away

When a giraffe runs fast it gallops. It puts both front legs on the ground while lifting its back legs. Then it brings both back legs to the ground ahead of its front legs, and almost immediately lifts its front legs again to take another large step, or stride. A rabbit gallops in the same way. Giraffe can reach speeds of 50 to 60 kilometres per hour when galloping.

Giraffe are sometimes a target for hungry lions.

Staying out of trouble

Giraffe use their excellent eyesight to stay out of trouble. Day or night, they can see when danger is near.

Because giraffe are so tall and big, they are not easy to catch. They also have a very powerful kick. But sometimes lions manage to catch giraffe. Some groups of lions have learnt how to hunt giraffe. The lions chase a giraffe over uneven ground, such as rocky slopes. The giraffe may trip and fall down, and then the lions attack it.

Newborn calves cannot run fast, so they hide in long grass until they have grown bigger. The calves' mothers watch over them and protect them from lions and hyenas. The mothers use their powerful kick to chase the predators away.

Calves grow quickly. The bigger and taller a calf is, the safer it is from many kinds of predators. So a calf grows one metre in the first six months of its life. That is a huge amount! And by the time the calf is a year old, it is already two metres tall. Even though some predators are stronger than a giraffe, predators tend to be frightened of the giraffe's size.

Giraffe lie down to rest at night, but they usually sleep for only five minutes at a time. They need to be **alert** so that they can get up and defend themselves in case a predator starts to attack them while they are sleeping.

Other animals, such as zebra, often feed near giraffe and rely on the giraffe to be on the lookout for danger.

Helping other animals

Because giraffe are tall and have good eyesight, many other animals stay close to them. The other animals watch the giraffe carefully. If the giraffe become frightened, this usually means that danger is near. The other animals will notice when the giraffe become alert and aware of danger, and they will run away.

Giraffe are curious animals. They like to know what is going on around them. For example, they watch carefully to see what other animals are doing. If a giraffe sees a cheetah lying in the grass, it will stare at it. Smaller animals, such as warthog or impala, notice that the giraffe is staring. They then realise that there is a predator in the area.

People visiting a game reserve sometimes find lion or cheetah by looking towards the spot where a giraffe is staring.

Warthogs often stay close to giraffe, trusting the much taller giraffe to notice any danger.

Giraffe sometimes make sounds to communicate with other giraffe.

Making a noise

Many people believe that giraffe are mute, or cannot make sounds. This is not true. Giraffe are mostly silent, but they are able to make sounds. Giraffe make many kinds of sounds to **communicate** with each other.

Every type of animal needs to make sounds to warn others when danger is near. The different warning sounds that a giraffe makes are snorts, bleats, mews, bellows and coughs. But because giraffe are mostly silent, people are lucky if they hear a giraffe making any of these sounds.

A giraffe's top lip bends easily and picks leaves off trees without being pricked by thorns.

How giraffe and thorny trees both stay healthy

Trees that grow in good soil produce healthy, **nutritious** leaves that taste good to browsers, including giraffes. But many nutritious plants grow thorns to stop giraffe and other browsers from eating *all* their leaves.

These thorns do not hurt the giraffe's lips or tongue. This is because the giraffe's tongue is rubbery and rough, and hair protects its lips from being pricked. Also, its long tongue and pointy lips help it to avoid the thorns while it is eating the leaves.

Giraffe need to eat a large amount of food every day to keep healthy. But the thorns on plants make it difficult for giraffe to eat the leaves, so they have to eat more carefully. For this reason, giraffe will look for another tree, one that has no thorns, and spend some time eating from it. In this way, both the thorny tree and the giraffe **benefit**. The giraffe eat only some of the thorny tree's nutritious leaves, and the thorny tree stays healthy by keeping most of its leaves.

Two female okapis. Okapi are members of the giraffe family.

Relatives

The only other member of the giraffe family is the okapi. Okapis live in the Democratic Republic of Congo, a country in central Africa. Okapis live in forests where there is a lot of rain. But when it rains, these animals do not stay wet for long. This is because there is oil in the okapis' fur, which makes the water run off their bodies.

The okapi has stripes on its legs, like a zebra, but the okapi's body is shaped like that of a giraffe. The okapi's neck is long, but not as long as a giraffe's neck.

Both the okapi and the giraffe have long tongues. These animals eat leaves, and they use their tongues to pull the leaves off trees. Like the giraffe, male okapi have short, bony horns that are covered with skin. They also have large ears that help them to hear when danger is near.

The giraffes' long-haired tail is one of the things for which people hunt giraffe.

Conservation

When we conserve wildlife, we protect wild animals and the places where these animals live.

The total number of giraffe left in Africa nowadays is about 80 000. There are many giraffe in Africa, and there are many kinds of giraffe.

Some kinds of giraffe are endangered, which means that there are only a few of them left in the wild. Two examples are the Rothschild's giraffe, which lives in Uganda, southern Sudan and western Kenya, and the West African giraffe. These giraffe may become extinct – soon there may be no more of them left in the world.

Giraffe have already become extinct in some countries in Africa, such as Burkina Faso, Eritrea, Guinea, Malawi, Mauritania and Senegal.

People hunt giraffe for their meat, skins and tails. The meat of a giraffe can feed a family for a long time. The long hairs in a giraffe's tail are used to make good-luck charms, or the whole tail may be used as a flyswatter. People also destroy the places where giraffe live by cutting down trees and setting up villages and towns.

Giraffe are not endangered in southern Africa. This is because most of them live in game reserves, where they are protected.

A giraffe bends down to drink water by spreading its front legs out sideways.

Glossary

adaptations – changes or special features in an animal's body that make it easier for the animal to live in its area

advantage – something that helps or gives a better chance

alert – quick to notice danger

associations – groups

benefit – to gain something that is useful

browsers – animals that eat leaves from trees

camouflage – the colours or patterns on an animal's coat that help the animal to blend in with plants and other things around it, so that it cannot be seen

communicate – to share information

Latin – the language that the ancient Romans spoke long ago

nutritious – good, healthy food

oestrus – the times when the female is ready to mate

predators – animals that hunt and kill other animals for food

skeletons – the sets of bones that support and hold up humans and animals' bodies

temporary – not permanent; for a short time

temporary associations – groups that stay together for a short time

territories – areas where an animal, or group of animals, lives

vulnerable – at risk of being attacked or harmed

www.ingramcontent.com/pod-product-compliance
Lightning Source LLC
Chambersburg PA
CBHW041323290426
44108CB00004B/110